FOCUS

Collections of Poetry by Donald Lev

HYN and Other Poems
A String of Beads for Maxine
Peculiar Merriment
Intercourse with the Dead
Footnotes
There Is Still Time
The Days of the Easter Bunny
Twentieth Century Limited
Twilight
Enemies of Time
Yesterday's News
Grief
Adventures at the Upstate—Poems on Films
The Darkness Above: Selected Poems 1968-2002
Only Wings—20 Poems of Devotion
A Very Funny Fellow
Where I Sit

Focus

Donald Lev

N̶Y̶Q̶ Books™

The New York Quarterly Foundation, Inc.
New York, New York

NYQ Books™ is an imprint of The New York Quarterly Foundation, Inc.

The New York Quarterly Foundation, Inc.
P. O. Box 2015
Old Chelsea Station
New York, NY 10113

www.nyq.org

First Edition

Set in New Baskerville

Layout by Victoria Eremo

Cover Design by Raymond P. Hammond

Cover Art: "Still Life with Pears," 16 × 20 in., oil on canvas by Rita Kaiser, 2017

Author Photo by Eldad Benary

Library of Congress Control Number: 2017934719

ISBN: 978-1-63045-036-6

Focus

Acknowledgements

Poems in this volume have previously appeared in the following publications: *The Same, The Iconoclast, Waterways, And Then, House Organ, Street Value, Chronogram, Home Planet News, CAPS Anthology, Home Planet News On Line.*

Contents

I. FOCUS ON GOD

II.PARTY TIME

III. HOW THINGS CAME TO BE

IV. EPILOGUE

To the poets of the Hudson Valley, for their warmth.

And in memory of Enid Dame—her continuous light.

I see in slow motion
Give details of details
Like a microscope
No wonder you don't read me...
Your eye isn't in me.

—*From "Faith" by Donald Lev*
HYN and Other Poems, *1968*

I. FOCUS ON GOD

FOCUS

I've been trying to put God in focus
As I plant myself in front of
Fans and air conditioners
Trying to keep cool.

I just got off the phone
With my oldest friend (with whom I hadn't
Spoken for a good 65 years till just now).

His mother used to pray for my conversion.

We spoke of friends who'd passed, and shingles, and
Families.

WE ARE SAFE HERE

We are safe here
Under this piece of tin.

The worst cannot approach
While the worse is in abeyance.

There are things to do.
We have brought our games

And a little bread and wine.

ST. PATRICK'S DAY

To celebrate St. Patrick's Day,
I watched *Gangs of New York,*
The film in which Martin Scorsese
Shows us that, however mean
The Italian streets of New York were,
The Irish ones were worse.
Which leads me to recall the time

The Mayflower dropped me off at Ellis Island,
Where Boss Tweed greeted me like a
Prodigal father, enrolled me in the Democratic Party,
And warned me against
A future of writing poetry and living off women;
Then turned me over to some German
Ladies from uptown

Who brought me to Temple Emanu-el,
Made me take a bath, learn Hebrew,
And study the lives of the great
German-Jewish philanthropists;
After which I moved to Queens,
Took up chess and began my
Close study of the Racing Form.

I'd gladly bring this narrative
Down to the present,
But I've lost the thread.

VOLUME ONE NUMBER ONE

We were all part of
Fred Meinholz's menagerie
That he began putting together
In the *New York Times* wire room
During World War II, when manpower was scarce.
We were alcoholics, epileptics, homosexuals,
Apprentice playwrights and hopeful players;
Mostly we were alcoholics. John, who happened to
Have grown up with my half-brother in
Hamden, Connecticut; Jack, a refugee from
An Edith Wharton novel who saw his
Family in Massachusetts the few times
A year when they chose to tolerate him,
And otherwise mainlined gin and read
Edith Wharton novels, and I worked the same
Menial job playing nursemaid
To teletype and cable machines,
Changing their rolls and sorting their papers;
After which the three of us would go drinking together
Up and down Eighth Avenue,
But mostly in the lounge of the sorry old hotel
Delmore Schwartz chose to end his life in
A few years later.

It has since become a welfare hotel,
And a homeless shelter, and has just been closed down.
After Fred died and a new regime took over the wire room,
We lost our jobs one by one, I being the last to go,
A permanent victim of the big strike of 1962.

John took up with a Scottish waitress and went to work
At the post office, and I think sobered up somewhat.
Jack had this huge apartment on the west side
Where he threw, or someone threw, decadent parties,
And then moved to the Upper East Side, where I saw him last.

This was 1969 and I was trying to raise funds for my
First magazine.

Jack was living with a tall, beefy, elegant
Man who wore his grey hair down to his waist, and who
Was a well-known designer of jewelry.
Anyway, I found myself seated between them,

And they were doing "poppers." They insisted I
Participate, and on the elevator speeding upward,
Or plunging downward, I realized
My hosts found my visit impertinent and were
In the process of murdering me.

I left, however, with a check for $250,
Enough in those days to launch Volume One Number One.

MINIMUM COMFORT

Woods.

I've never felt quite safe in them.
I'm from a place called Forest Hills,
Which boasted neither forests nor hills

Though I witnessed a hit and run accident once
On Queens Boulevard, where
Because of all the traffic one forgets
There is occasional limited vision
Due to paved-over hills.
There were thickets not far from where I lived,
Where I'd spend many of my truancies.

Sometimes I'd see a hare flash by.
Once I saw a frozen cat.
But as for real woods.

Enid and I
Were looking at a house once
Fairly deep in the woods around
Kerhonkson.

It had eerie stone stairs
And cellars.

And the only nearby commercial
Place was a convenience store called
Duffy's.

I figured that geopolitically
To survive there you would have
To be on good terms with Duffy.

And if you weren't?
But the real woods are scary, full of
Sharp-snouted animals
And natives with feathers stuck in their scalps
And war paint, who
Probably blame everything on the Jews
And Protestants with big hats and
Sunburnt faces, who pretend friendliness
But sneer at your awkward struggles
With the underbrush.

No, I need to see
A public building or two just for
Minimum comfort.

HISTORY LESSON

That election of 1864
If I know myself at all,
I'd say I'd have voted
For the peace candidate,
George B. McClellan.

You can't win 'em all!

GLOBETROTTING

I thought I might make a little journey
To a movie theater showing a foreign film
That would not be long in the area.
But I just couldn't raise the ambition to
Lift my carcass out of the not that
Comfortable chair in the café I was in
To set off. But then a group of Italian-speaking
Tourists came in—three muscular young men
And a rather lithe young woman.

They ordered sandwiches which the men
Began masticating masculinely as only
European men do, and pointing with their sandwiches
To the paintings on the wall, rapidly
Critiquing them in their dialect,
While I began imagining the English subtitles.
A little later, an acquaintance of mine
Sat himself down and apropos of nothing
Informed me he would soon
Be flying to Italy to "look at houses" for friends of his.
I thought, gee, I would like to be able to
Say something like that, but to say it,
I guess I would have to do it, which I
Would probably be reluctant to.

ROOT

It was totally dark. I couldn't see.
I stumbled over the root of a giant tree
And fell to the ground, ground that was rolling.
I held on to that root as the earth turned beneath me.
I clutched the twirling planet in both arms as it seemed
To be flung in the direction of a gigantic batsman.
"Oh no!" I screamed as the batter swung and missed;
And I suffered the happy crushing leather sting
Of the catcher's mitt. The crowd roared and I rejoiced.

UKRAINIAN WEDDING

I couldn't do it today: hold that crown,
That heavy gold or silver or brass
Crown over the bride's head
The whole way down the aisle.

But the bride's gangster father
Stood glaring at me lest I fail.

Later he confided to me, apologetically,
That I didn't have to carry the crown up high,
That he had been remembering his wedding
When the crown was cardboard, not metal.

Still it was one of my life's few proud moments,
When I carried the crown that well.

TREASURE

Here's a program signed by Joey Lapchik.
Another signed by Tony Leswick.
Still others signed by Dolph Shayes, Kid Gavilan, Terry Saw-
chuk.

A postcard signed by Maybelle, June, Anita, and Helen Carter.
Another by Hank Williams.

A scrapbook full of news photos from the 1951
National League playoff between the Dodgers and the Giants.

Autographs too. Bobby Thomson, Hank Thompson, Willie Mays,
Eddie Stanky, Leo Durocher, Sal Maglie, to name a few.

Quite a trove, my mother discovered in my closet one day
And threw into the second floor incinerator chute.

THE DAYS OF THE BIG BANDS

The big Base dance
Was to be tonight
And I still didn't have a date.
I was short and ugly
But I had an agile brain,
So I moseyed over to the
Nurses' tent
To offer them up my blood.

This led to the most scintillating banter,
And I wound up dancing to the beat
Of Kay Kyser
With the vivacious nurse
Beatrice (Va Va Voom) van Bloom.
That was the war for me.
I hope it was as good for you.

Only thing, everyone
Always used to try to act officiously.

They still do.
Don't you find that too?

DEATH BEFORE DISHONOR...

Was some sort of regimental motto, I suppose.
The kid wore it tattooed over his healthy biceps.
He'd been AWOL a long, long time,
Just hanging around the neighborhood.

You could see he was terrified.
He must have had a premonition.
They caught up with him
And sent him directly to Viet Nam.

They must have given him his choice
Between that and the brig.

In Viet Nam he did not long live.

OCTOBER

October. Month so
Many choose to die in.
Across the road
A young woman is dying.
Her numerous family
Has gathered to be with her,
Causing a parking problem
For me. Poor me. I have been nagging
The supermarket for weeks
To replenish their supply of yahrtseit
Candles. Today they did, so I
Purchased my year's supply
For both my October and my later dead.

I said to my dying neighbor's father,
"God be with you," surprising myself.
I wondered what I meant by "God."
Something, perhaps, more than can be
Talked about, less than can be said.

IT'S GIUSEPPE VERDI'S BIRTHDAY
10/10/13

It's Giuseppe Verdi's birthday
And I'm celebrating by pulling out
My favorite Verdi opera,
La Forza Del Destino,
In a box of vinyl records featuring
My all-time favorite soprano
Renata Tebaldi, as Leonora.

Her voice my image of importance in life.

And I gather at the death scenes of
Leonora, Aida, Violetta,
With sobbing, impotent swains,
And know, as Verdi's music knows.

CHRISTOPHER COLUMBUS

Christopher Columbus has gotten
A terrible press in recent years.

Lord knows he's earned it. But wait.
Ought one of us of European descent
Really, in good conscience, to
Join fellow citizens with such alacrity
In contempt of him whom legend has it led us here?

In New York City there used to be and still may be
Two Columbus Day parades: one Italian and one Hispanic.
I remember once watching the Italian one on television
And the announcer giving greeting to favored paraders
Along the march and invariably ending each greeting with
"Be Proud!" I found this "Be Proud!" so touching.

Some of us may remember how negatively
Each sequence of immigration was often greeted
By those who preceded them to these shores.
There was a saying among those of my particular
Bands of marauders when things didn't work out well:
"Ah klug on Columbus"—a curse on Columbus.
I'm sure the saying preceded our learning
The fates of our people who stayed behind.

Columbus did bad things to people he found here.
And people fitting our general racial description
Did bad things to people not fitting our general racial description.

This is history and we cannot wish it away.
To be honest is to acknowledge it
And even in some sense embrace it.
And be proud!

THE GLORY OF THE JEWISH PEOPLE

I'm talking Bugsy Siegel and Meyer Lansky,
Who made the deserts of Nevada to bloom
With gambling casinos and first-class entertainment.

I know those hypocrites in *Eretz Israel*
Turned Meyer away when he tried to claim
The so-called "law of the return."

Well, fuck them!
The only Promised Land of the Jewish People
Or probably any people
Is the good old U. S. of A.

Don't get me started.
I'm talking about the glory of the Jewish People:
Meyer Lansky, Bugsy Siegel,
My uncle Dave, my great uncle Jack.

I know the last two are small fry
I'm trying to put with the big shots.
Well, it's my family and my fucking poem,
So if Bugsy and Meyer have anything to say,
They know where to find me.

"NEVER WISEN UP A CHUMP..."

A saying amongst my father and his
Contemporaries (he was born in 1901)
Which I have been conscious of
My whole life
But only came to realize yesterday
That the "chump" was me.

WHITE PLAINS

I remember him breathing noisily
Though diving with much authority.

I remember a car full of fumes, though
I would not have known enough to call them fumes
At the time, and becoming carsick.

Not long after
My uncle Harry had a
Big heart attack
Driving home from a funeral.

He was an interior decorator with tacks in his mouth;
Lived in Westchester with family
Including my aunt Florence and my two cousins;
Was thought of as prosperous.

He drove with authority; spoke with authority.
His whole family, excepting my aunt, died young.

GAZA

Isn't that where that temple was
That that Israeli giant Samson
Pulled down over his head
And the heads of half the Philistines?

THE HUMAN RACE AND ME

They have these cunning little minds
Always thinking ahead.

I almost never think ahead.

PACKAGING

The dying.

The recently expired.

Their caretakers, their mourners.

This poem is in homage
To all

The poetry
Packaged in love and loss.

MY MOST RECENT HAUNTING

There was one chair.
The ghost chose to sit there.
I didn't think ghosts needed to sit,
And I said this. The ghost pretended
Not to hear. We sat on opposite sides
Of the room and pretended to ignore each other.
"As a haunting, this is pretty boring,"
I dared to think. At this, the ghost disappeared.

ON SELF MANAGEMENT

The time the management
Of the agency I was
Running messages for
Suggested I get a pager,
I asked, "So you can own me?"

There's something I'm trying to say
Concerning The Public and The Private
That is probably too late to say today.

BUSINESS

I moved my chair a little
So the sun and I would not so directly
Confront each other.

It was that important a meeting.

A LITTLE POEM FOR PRESIDENTS' DAY

The worst thing was
I was allergic to the
Powder in my powdered whig.
How my cabinet used to
Avert their eyes
When I went into one of my
Sneezing jags.
Otherwise, being an early President
Wasn't so bad. Not in retrospect.

RANDOM LYRIC

We're in the future now,
We're in the future now.
We used to be in the Past,
            But at last
We're in the future now!

THAT VOICE

1.
That voice
Rising above everybody's.

I can't hear what it says. I'm furious.

2.
I try to listen
To you and the others,
But the voice I hate
And do not listen to

I follow.

3.
I thought I heard an elephant cry out
For food sex freedom water.

I thought I heard my self cry out
For none of these things.
.

MY DAY

One idea was collecting words from,
I don't know, anywhere, the past most probably,
And make sense of them.
But I kept knocking them off the desk
And the light was so bad
I couldn't find them to
pick them up so
With such a limited vocabulary...

Then this car I was about to enter
Was rammed by another car,
Which was my car.

And worse,
I got up so early today
It isn't even lunchtime.

ALONG THE SIDE

Come along the side of the house
Where there used to be a path.
Remember the Euphrates, as I dubbed
The stream of clear water that had originated
From a broken pipe so long ago.
You might find Enid's Lilith sitting sadly
Between the jewel weed and the bee balm,
Waiting for Messiah to come
Drive her to a nursing home.

CHARTER

I found myself struggling to fight my way
Out from under a mountain of
Indescribably assorted trash.

I burrowed, I flailed,
I dug, and I kicked, till I clawed my way free.
At last I was free of politics!

I looked around and saw nothing.
Do you know what nothing looks like?
Neither do I, because nothing looks like nothing.

NUMBER ONE

When we were number one
We could wave away our enemies
With one strong arm, then roll back to sleep
In blankets as comfortable as graves.
When we were number one we controlled the waves
Of the sea and the sneezes and wheezes of men.

When we were number one, there was no need of sobriety.

Now, there is no need of sobriety.

THE NEW MOVEMENT IN THEATER

We're just all sitting here waiting
For something to happen.

You didn't exactly promise anything,
But expectations grow sometimes, or maybe
All the time, anyway.

I feel like I'm fifteen again,
Hanging on the corner outside Rikers
Doing nothing, with some other kids
Doing the same.

"Where's everybody?" one of us asks.
Another answers, "I dunno. City, maybe."

Now six characters in search of six other characters
Mount the stage.
Oh, this is going to be good, I feel.

II.PARTY TIME

PARTY TIME

Beheadings in Saudi Arabia draw large crowds.
No surprise. Public executions have always
Been well attended, from drawings and quarterings
In Merry Olde England and its colonies
To the lynchings in 19th and 20th century USA.

I am amazed and gratified by my
Country's maturity, when I reflect that reality TV
Has not yet launched The Execution Channel
For its potentially avid viewers.

THE FOG

Fog dropped down on everything.
The queen, checking to see
Whether her favorite stallion
Was well enough shod,
Was no exception.

She was obliterated
With the rest of history.

I closed all my windows
And switched all my lights on
So I was not obliterated.
Everything else was.

PREPARING MY ROLE

I tried my best to find the motivation
Of the character I was to portray:
An arthritic gaffer who drank wine all day,
Talked to himself, and wrote
Little poems that were poorly disguised
Complaints about his personal aches and pains.

I couldn't find any motivation,
So I just winged it.

BOXING DAY

It is Boxing Day
And I am in the ring
With Max Schmeling.

We're in a clinch and he keeps
Apologizing for Hitler,
But also keeps pounding me.

I know he is a more
Experienced boxer than I am
But he is 109 years old
And I am only 78
And I hate losing to such an old guy.

MARIO

We don't have that much to boast about in Queens.
The term, a little odious, a little wistful, "outer borough"
Was really coined for Queens, which lacked the
Panache of Brooklyn, the raw intellectualism of The Bronx,
The utter indecipherable mysteriousness of Staten Island.

Sir Mario Cuomo riding into the wilds west of Lefrak City
On missions of peace he accomplishes bravely.
A knight he was, both wise and just.
That's a way I like to remember Governor Mario Cuomo.

ROOFING IT

When my fate landed on the roof
Of my apartment house
It did some damage
To the wall the landlord had just had built
To keep children from falling off.

But people who came to the roof to wait on fate
Did not usually go near the edge.

They were less interested in what was happening
Above below and around them
Than within their tiny brain spaces.

That's how I remember leaving New Jersey.
Some of my stuff was moved to High Falls by
Zen Movers.

Whether by surface or air is immaterial.

EYELASHES

Long brown eyelashes
Brown pensive eyes
Hair dark, gypsy,
She was like a pirate queen.

Even when I walked in on her and her
Gang of thieves counting up their loot
From cigarette and milk machines
And I had to tell them to get the hell out
I couldn't help but love her

The pirate queen.

Months later, in San Francisco
She called the police, told them
She was afraid of me.
I was fast asleep when they came to arrest me.
They threw me in the drunk tank
And next day
The judge strongly suggested I leave town.

When I told milady, she broke into tears.

UP MY SLEEVE

Something up my sleeve.
I think it's lettuce.
This organic tomato
I found behind your ear
Should not disappear
But contribute to the salad
That my brain is turning into.

A little celery onion and anchovy
Wouldn't hurt. Maybe pitted olives.

And Newman's Own dressing of course
So we feel helpful a little.

VALENTINES DAY

First I got to get over to that garage on North Clark Street,
Meet with some other guys, do some business.
Then we'll get together at that
Nice little restaurant you like
And, you know, eat some oysters.

DOORJAMBALAYA

After scratching my back on the doorjamb
I proceeded inside and fell into the nearest chair
Wherefrom I began to plot my evening's
Assault on time: beer? wine? vodka? rum?

"Jambalaya crawfish pie…"

Crawfish. I'd identify with that if it was a crawl fish.
Which it isn't.

I know my ichthyology like I know my carpentry.

But something that crawls: that would be me,
Around sills or thresholds, till caught in a spider's web.

But crawl I don't. Scratching my back
Drew this long splinter.

I sat in my chair bleeding onto the floor.
I chose rum.

Hank's next cut was "Settin' the Woods on Fire."

THE IDES OF MARCH
3/15/15

I'm hanging around in the shadows
Of the Capitol
Hoping certain of my colleagues
Won't spot me. They're
Putting together a committee to
Well, they say, to hit the President with a
Stun gun and take him somewhere to reason with him
Till he sees things our way.

I know there's something wrong with this plan,
But I just don't think it's time to share my doubts.

THE ONLY WAY

I am on stage, spotlighted mercilessly.
All around is total darkness.
I have been assured there is an audience,
But if there is, it is very quiet. No applause, not a cough.
I try this dumb gag that usually works as an icebreaker.
Nothing.

I try everything I have, including singalongs.
I even organize three-part harmonies,
Assigning different parts to different
Areas of the unlit theater.

Still no evidence of an audience in the darkness,
But I feel persistence
Is the only way open to me.

PLAN

I drove my car into a ditch. I got out
And that was that.

I needed a whole list of things
But had no list.

Worry seemed a good enough plan right then.
Besides, it was getting chilly.

LONESOME JACK

At the end of a barely beaten path
There is a dark place amid half-barren trees.
No one's there yet. Several are expected
To come memorialize Lonesome Jack,
Who had himself buried there
A year ago last spring.

Now it is fall and we'll try not to fail him.

ENTELECHY

For Rudy Scherreiks

From Earth's rocks
The super-heroic geologist
On viewless wings rises
To the place where divine mischief
Is to be prevented or reversed.

Imagine such a battle!
I can't.

But I can see possibility
As ants gather at the bottom of a juice glass,
Or when a summer afternoon stillness
Brings tears.

IDLING

Where is that singing coming from?
And is it a song of welcoming or dismissal,
Of embracing or letting go?

Is it just wind in the trees, or birdcall?
Is it sound at all, or just the mind's playing?

IN THE MIDDLE

Sitting in the middle of a rainstorm
That blasts as if from a showerhead
Just on me.

I can't move.
I can't see.

But the rest of the world is dry.
This I know.

STEP BY STEP

My doctor—a good guy,
Just trying to look out for me,

Suggested I just open my back door
And piss in my backyard.

I didn't know how to explain to him
That, coming from Queens,
I just couldn't do that.

Whatever they did in those
Uncouth other boroughs
Which we came to Queens to escape
We could hardly wish to emulate.

So I pull myself slowly step by step
Up old wooden stairs
And by and by arrive, most times in time.

THE LATEST NEWS

Reminds me of the day
I'd been sleeping on the floor
Of a house in San Francisco
After a night of indulgence
In the ever-flowing waters
Of Red Mountain Burgundy.

I woke up shaking.
I thought it was the death rattle
And that the Angel of Death had come for me.

But it was only an earthquake—a very minor one—
Much too small to concern
That particular Angel at that particular time

ABOARD THE AFRICAN QUEEN

I must be Humphrey
And you, whom
I no longer see, but
Know your presence, must of course be Kate.

Things race
To uncontrollable conclusion

After which we must right ourselves.
We must.

WRITER

I kept writing it all down.
Whatever was read,
Whatever was said,
At every writers' conference,
I'd write it.

Strong tea,
If you ask me.

LATE RENAISSANCE

A Black Widow spider

In a sack of organic plums

From Medici Farms.

FOLK SONG

What are we to do, Mister?
What are we ever to do?

You told us one thing yesterday
And you told us another thing today.

What are we to do, Mister?
What are we ever to do?

POUR IT

My father used to tell bartenders
"You pour it, I'll drink it."

His prayer.

SATORI

Eyes open
On half of a pint glass of beer
And one wasabi nut.

BIBLE LESSON

In honor of the good people of Emanuel AME Church, Charleston, S.C.

If you ask for little,
You get less.
It says something like that in Holy Scripture,
In the "new" part of that big book,
Written in pretty depressing times of course,
When pessimism seemed the most practical response.

Now travel ahead in time to the good old U.S.A.,
Maybe to that section that was once the good old C.S.A.
Imagine sitting among other interested people discussing
That same strange, still controversial book, when in walks a nice
Looking young person who isn't even one of you
But seems to like you and reads the Bible,
and you make Him welcome.

Now, those of you who've survived his crime forgive him?

ESTORIL

For Victoria Sullivan

Back in ancient times,
When I was a boy,
And there were still monarchs
Sovereign enough to depose,

I'd dream of hanging out with them,
The sad, rich, ex-kings,
So full of loss and sin.

Of course I don't mean really
Ancient times like those of
Cheops or Akhnaton—a little
Mysterious for my taste, and I'm afraid
Akhnaton would bore me with his
Incessant religious chatter.

But King Farouk! There's one
I'd love to see: roly-poly Farouk,
His tall fez teetering dangerously
From his wronged and royal head.

Perhaps he'd come down for a visit
To King Carol, Admiral Horthy,
And the rest of the gang, and me.

We'd have such a lively chat
About jewels and horses
And replacements for knees.

BREAK IN THE LINE OF DUTY

Always joked around,
Had a good word for everybody.

He'll be missed.

VARIATION ON A PIECE OF CLASSIC AMERICAN SONG-CRAFT

Somewhere over the rainbow,
Pit bulls bite…

RETURNING THE FLAVOR

Under warm umbrellas of revered beaches,
Above the seashells, the fortresses,
The cleansing, salty power
Playing on the shore;

Sending scent of Sabretts, Needicks, Hebrew National,
Sauerkraut, mustard, beer, and Gabilas Delicious Knishes,
Dancing back seaward in a pungent summer cloud.

IT'S NEVER TOO LATE

Us 79-year-olds
Are taking over.

They wouldn't let us before,
But now all them old bastards are gone.

THEATER PROJECT

NOT AN EXIT
Is my reworking
Of a depressing Sartre chestnut.

SOMEBODY OUT THERE

Greetings from the Universe
To the ruling species
of the so-called Planet Earth:

We warmly invite your participation
In the work of our many multi-astral
Organizations and institutions
Which, believe me, will bring you
Many advantages. But

To join us you must part
With all your absurd weapons,
Including pesticides.

(By the way, the concept "pest"
Needs explaining. Who has the right
To call who the pest?)

Of course you may refuse to join
The Intergalactic Community,

But then you'll have to get used to
Doing without those
Silly satellites of yours.

NEW YORK, TUESDAY, JULY 28, 2015

No poemable thought has arrived today
With today's *New York Times*

Though Hilary's head and shoulder shot
That dares front Old Glory

Might make something
For someone to say.

HAILED

Broadway,
Heading down from Columbus Circle,
Close to show time.
Maybe it has just stopped raining.
You notice,
But for only a moment
You are amidst
As great beauty as there is.
You are hailed. It is over.
You and your fare are off to the theater.

GOLD & SILVER

I stood back from the bar and contemplated
My freshly poured pint of golden brew
Next to which my shot of glacial vodka
Expressed such amour
As is only found among the greater elements.

YELLOW BIRDS

These big yellow birds
Sitting on a branch
Screaming the blues

It was hard enough
Thinking of anything else
With that going on

There was something I had to do
Something I needed to write down
But I had to let it all go.

STRATAGEM

Sorry I thought
You were talking to me
But it was that little phone you were talking into,
Your warm passionate breaths
Entering that
Small device.

THE FIRST QUESTION

The first question
The first questioner asked
Was a good one though
Not a great question
Such as the more professional
Second questioner might ask
If you were permitted past
The first questioner
Who was showing a
Confused though stubborn grasp.

III. HOW THINGS CAME TO BE

HOW THINGS CAME TO BE: BOOK ONE

I lay on my back
Balancing a glass of juice of some
Kind on my chest,
Contemplating the universe, its
Beginnings, at least as far back
As a kind of kindergarten for angels
Where Satan was the worst little angel and
Michael was the second worst.
This is where the Big Bang happened.
No wonder. That's as far as I got.

DETAILS

Like watching your
Own life
Diminish
Upon the monitor
The hospital sets up
To track your oxygen levels.

I have no love for details.
A new doctor I have just been visiting
Handed me a questionnaire asking
How many drinks I had today,
How many yesterday,
And how many the day before.

I know that the most
Superb artists
Are masters of description,
Sticklers for detail.

But a little spittle here,
A puff of smoke there,
And worlds are suggested.

Works for me.

ONE OF THOSE STORIES

I was sick of the sound of sword play.
My nerves were scratched thin.
I had to get away,
Which meant leaving my only friends,

Porthos, Athos, Aramis and D'Artagnan.

WAIT TILL I WIPE MY TEARS AWAY

Wait till I wipe my tears away.
I may have something to say.
Like this might have been,
Or that should not have been.

THE NOT SO GREAT

I escaped.
I thought that would
Make me feel good.
Free, anyway. Everyone
Wants freedom!

But I found myself in such
Gloom, such eternal bleak drizzle,
I turned myself in. Needless to say,
They didn't want me back.

ROLLING

There it is rolling.
Roll it will where it will
Till stopped.
One peers through the cool leafy
Theater
At this
And wonders whether to be glad or not.

SNUFFED

The candle snuffed, I slept.
A point at which it is difficult
To locate additional phenomena
Without "I awakening,"
Which I do not wish yet to occur,
Or dreaming, which, come on!
Has been done.

So let me plunge into it.
It is nothing, but
There is nothing beside.
You can no more feel it than see it
But there is nothing beside it.

A ROAD

I pass this family hurrying down
The road I'm struggling up.
They, a young couple, are walking briskly,
Their little boy is trotting beside them
Trying to keep hold of his father's hand.

They head toward the sound of a band,
And people, sunshine, frivolity.
I am heading home for a search
For something I will not find
And a labor of love gone grimly cold.

CHILL

Chill went through the entire attic.
Stacks of things grinned quizzically
In the eerie light.

I began my researches without clue,
Hoping something I'd blow dust off
Would end them.

A LATE WORK

Then the crows stopped conversing,
The angels stopped lecturing,
And there was a great silence
Broken only by a scraping.

Then there was only the scraping.
It lasted one half hour
After which I thought I heard
Myself trying to say
"I am lost."

PATCHES

Nothing's very clear.
Maybe what weather forecasters
Mean by patchy fog.
Thing to do is try to see
Between patches,
A leaf here, a twig there,
A cat with a bird in his mouth,
A parked minivan.

SWEEPING

I set myself sweeping.
It was about time.
You wouldn't believe
The trash I collected,
All the advice on how
To live and even
How to die,
Along with invitations to luncheons
To discuss such matters.

TRANSCENDING

Last time I tried
Transcending myself

I landed at the bottom
Of a hill amongst

A lot of rocks and wires
And nails and stuff.

But that doesn't mean
I'll stop trying.

INTERVIEW WITH A SCHOLAR

One candle lighted
A room of bookshelves.

The shelves were filled
With books alright.

I tried to remember what books
Were on them, if any of the books were mine.

There wasn't enough light to read the titles.
So I just thumbed through a copy of *People*
Magazine and waited for the interviewee

Who claimed he wanted to do research
In 20th Century poetry,
But could only work at night.

And he asked whether he could
Move in some furniture
In case he got caught working late.

HOME BREW

It is something I created in my bathtub.
Try some. I have aged it to perfection, I think,
Though one can't be absolutely certain of such things.

The ingredients, while not exactly secret, are unobtainable,
Since they have disappeared entirely from my memory.

Perhaps they'll be recallable with tasting. I'm so glad you've come.
I've waited so long to sample this. I never drink alone.

LEAPING THE BERKSHIRES

I rushed through the museum,
Almost knocking over a bronze goddess
Looking for the one little room
That housed the only North American collection
Of ancient rubber bands.

It's wonderful living in The Berkshires,
Where you can leap from art show
Right into Donald Trump's production of *Coriolanus*
At Shakespeare & Company.

SOMETHING TO DO

Looking for something to do?
Something that will suit you,
Like writing a poem? You could try
Drinking. That works usually.
Sadly, cleaning or
Picking stuff off the floor
Won't do it; any more
Than finishing laying out
The magazine issue you're
Two years late with already.

SPACE

Something's gone haywire in the engine room.
I have to get back on the bridge,
Order an all-systems alert.
But I can't get out of bed.
When at last I do get out of bed
It'll be to find myself
Lost in space one more day.

DRUMS

Drums there were
But no one to pound them;
Horns un-blown
And piles of untuned strings.

All the musicians have gone.
Birds fly, but refuse to sing.
"Why?" we might ask. But don't.

BIG BOWL

Along the road called Via del Sol
We passed what looked like a gigantic bowl.
We climbed a little higher and saw
That it was indeed a bowl of pea soup
With a stalk of celery planted tree-like
In its center.

Further along
Were five-foot-tall toads and deer
With human faces and meadow larks
With sleepy eyes and lasciviously
Twisted beaks, but nothing (don't you agree?)
Was so poetically significant as that

Big bowl of soup with the celery tree.

LETTER ON LITTER

A littering problem
Could present itself as a literary problem:
A number of possibilities for word collages;
Or the option of pasting an entire area of litter
Down where it lies, shellacking it,
And Bravo! A commission fulfilled.

GIVING THANKS

Across the road I could see
Groups of pilgrims gathering 'round long wooden tables.

Some of them wore blankets, some wore caftans,
Others trench coats. There were veiled ones, masked ones
and bearded ones.
And lots of bratty children.

Piled on the tables were turkeys and chipmunks
Waiting to be butchered and shared,
And big jugs of applejack to help the pilgrims give thanks.

ROCK LYRIC

Terrorism's just another word
For nothing left to lose...

MY STORY

What's the use of telling my story?
Everyone's got their own story.
No one cares to hear how I climbed
Out of that hole one day and just knew
I was headed straight for Broadway.

Not *the* Broadway, but Broadway, Kingston,
Where my first start-up was launched
Offering the public hard-to-find
Delicatessen delicacies like
Stuffed derma and roasted turkey tusheys.

As every entrepreneur knows,
The road to Success is paved with failure.
Things have changed much for the better
Since I've gotten into the outdoor garment
And camping gear business;

Especially since we introduced
Our new line of suicide belts
Which is moving like fireworks.

APHORISM FOR HANUKKAH

It is better to light a candle *and* curse the darkness.

BIRD HAIKU

We've got a duty to History:
Try to catch it,
Try to keep it.

POEM

Deep
Behind
It sings past you
As you try to read
Your own mind.

It has flown. Let it fly.
If it lands, let it land.

HEY

I yelled "Hey!"
You were stretching off a top rung of a
Not very squarely placed ladder
And you turned when you heard me
And that I suppose made you fall and break
Your back and be handicapped the rest of your life.
I feel like hell for yelling "Hey!"
Though I pass your house without stopping every day.

THE NATURE OF HIS CRIME

This world I've inhabited—
Maybe a little too long—
I've never understood.

Case in point:

Pete Rose bet money
On his own team.

Can anyone enlighten me
As to the nature
Of his crime?

SPANISH WINE

I'm drinking Spanish wine, which I'm partial to,
And thinking of Spain—Hemingway's Spain—the only
Spain
I care to know. *The Sun Also Rises* is my preference
But *For Whom the Bell Tolls* will do. Actually,
I've never re-read either of them, and never will.
But scriptural truth do they each contain. As, for instance,
Jake to Lady Brett: "Wouldn't it be pretty to think so."

WHAT HAPPENS

In the silence
Waiting to be filled
You can almost hear

An egg explode,
A ring implode,
A leaf of paper fall;

And a call to prayer
Direct from Heaven.

VEGETATION

Vegetation grown wild upon her grave,
Imaging my own dereliction.

I'll set my heart a spell on emptiness;
Give it a rest.

WHAT ONE WANTS FROM ART

The dark column
I suppose is a tree.
There are mountains
And there is some sky.
But where is the sea?
I'm in the mood for sea
To float my raft on,
To anchor my hopelessness in.

THE WORKSHOP

Maybe you just didn't do it right.
Did you hold it straight out in front of your chest?
Were your elbows unbent?
Were your eyes open or closed?
There is a difference between great art and yours.
We've got to find out what it is.

IV. EPILOGUE

PARABLE

There was once this huge
Sorrowful fish
Who had just swallowed the last
Of the less huge fish
And was feeling lonely and suicidal.

He'd give anything to be caught
In one of those huge nets
And hauled gasping onto shore.

But there were no longer any nets.

END RHYMES

The arm wrestlers sat straining
While it started raining.

All that was soiled came clean:
Shoes that were muddied,
Feet that were bloodied,
Rust on a cracked canteen.
One rhyme for village
Is pillage.

One for hope
Is cope.

THE PERIMETER

Beyond the perimeter where the circle of light ended
Was such darkness as would seem nonexistence.

I, or someone or something pretending to a self like mine,
Entered into it, and began

A search for the finish line.

MY FINAL PLAY

The spotlight falls upon an otherwise
Totally darkened stage revealing
A park bench with me seated upon it.
I am mumbling something incoherent
As images of court rooms with murder
Trials going on in them play all around me.
I begin drawing pages of newsprint from
Under my clothing.

              I try to read them,
But it's no use. I toss them into the darkness
Whence I draw a laptop, which I place
Upon my lap as the curtain descends.
When the curtain rises, I take no bow.

FOOTSTONE

There's nothing
Not funny.

The New York Quarterly Foundation, Inc.

New York, New York

Poetry
Magazine

Since 1969

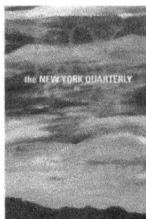

Edgy, fresh, groundbreaking, eclectic—voices from all walks of life.

Definitely NOT your mama's poetry magazine!

The *New York Quarterly* has been defining the term contemporary American poetry since its first craft interview with W. H. Auden.

Interviews • Essays • and of course, lots of poems.

www.nyq.org

No contest! That's correct, NYQ Books are NO CONTEST to other small presses because we do not support ourselves through contests. Our books are carefully selected by invitation only, so you know that NYQ Books are produced with the same editorial integrity as the magazine that has brought you the most eclectic contemporary American poetry since 1969.

Books

www.nyq.org

poetry at the edge™

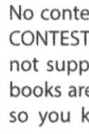
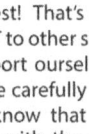
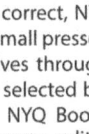
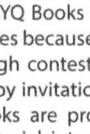
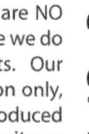

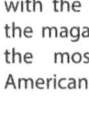
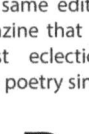
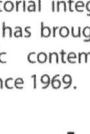

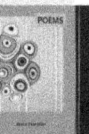

DONALD LEV was born in New York City in 1936. He attended Hunter College, worked in the wire rooms of the *Daily News* and *New York Times,* and then drove a taxi cab for 20 years (with a 6-year hiatus in which he ran messages for, and contributed poetry to, *The Village Voice* and operated the Home Planet Bookshop on the Lower East Side). His earliest poems appeared in print in 1958 and he started his first small press magazine, *HYN Anthology,* in 1969. Among his honors have been a Madeline Sadin Award from *New York Quarterly* in 1973 and a Life Time Achievement Award from the Catskill Reading Society/Outloudbooks in 2003. He was Distinguished Visiting Poet for the Northeast Poetry Center in Sugar Loaf, NY in July of 2012. In 2008 Outloudbooks brought out his *The Darkness Above: Selected Poems 1968-2002* a sampling from the first four decades of his writing. A chapbook, *Only Wings: 20 Poems of Devotion* was published in 2010 by Presa Press in Michigan, and a new collection, *A Very Funny Fellow,* was brought out by NYQ Books in February, 2012. His most recent book, *Where I Sit,* was published by Presa Press in 2015. His brief underground film-acting career pinnacled with his portrayal (he wrote his own lines) of "The Poet" in Robert Downey Sr.'s 1969 classic *Putney Swope.* He lives in High Falls, NY, where he publishes the literary tabloid *Home Planet News,* which he and his late wife Enid Dame founded in 1979.

www.ingramcontent.com/pod-product-compliance
Lightning Source LLC
Chambersburg PA
CBHW022010080426
42733CB00007B/555